Learning

for people who prefer not to be taught

F

G

I

When you've just met 2, 15, 17, 18, 23, 24, 32, 60, 64, 67, 79, 95, 102, 103, 125, 132, 148, 158, 159, 171, 189, 226, 230

When you're losing them 12, 21, 42, 44, 59, 74, 82, 102, 109, 132, 143, 171, 186, 203, 213, 218, 226, 230

Add categories you find useful

Editor's notes

> 'If everybody dared to be honest with each other all the time, our present school system would collapse very rapidly.'
> – The Little Red Schoolbook

The manual you are holding in your hands is incomplete.

It does not feature well-formulated lesson plans,
a history of art education or a step-by-step guide on how to set up your own radical education co-op.

It's a messy collection of ideas: contributions our friends and colleagues sent us, our own learning experiences and rumours we heard.

You might ask yourself who this manual is for. Is it for teachers? Is it for students? Is it only relevant for teaching art?

The answer is: Yes and No.

We don't know.

Probably both.

As self-employed artists, we have become used to performing our services anywhere, for anybody who books us. One day we might be doing a happy crafty afternoon in a primary school, the next day a post-graduate seminar on exhibition-making, the day after we're making soup for the reading group we organised. And our methodologies need to work in all of these contexts.

So this manual has come out of the frustration and the joy of never having what our grandmothers would call 'a permanent position'.

It has come out of years of being on-call teachers, troubleshooters, assistants. Working on one-year contracts that never get extended. Travelling for 2 days to give a 45-minute lecture. Grading students according to criteria we disagree with. Waiting for months to get paid (and only getting paid after threatening legal action).

Being a zero-hours-contract teacher is extremely isolating. You just come in, deliver, go home. There's no safety net, no solidarity. There is also no continuity. You will have very intimate conversations with people you'll never see again.

We started compiling this manual because we became afraid that we were losing our ability to care.

Once you've been 'in education' for a while, it's easy to become cynical. To talk about 'my students' as if you owned them. To dish out the standard advice phrases.

So this manual is a printed reminder of our impractical ideals. We made it to remind ourselves why we are angry about current education systems, norms and hierarchies.

We made this manual, because we got bored of providing content for the ubiquitous formats of hyper-individualised-tutorials, success-story-lectures, half-the-class-is-on-their-iphone-group-crits.

This manual encourages us to find out what happens if we don't deliver. If we don't give students the standard slide show, but instead make them take off their socks and rub their feet with mustard.

We know that spicy feet will not be an instant salvation, but we believe in going outside, in using our bodies and not only our brains, in absurd interventions, in silly jokes, in creating atmospheres, in learning in the gap, in destabilising our position, in talking about money.

We believe in letting things go so wrong that thinking about them ten years later still makes our stomachs hurt.

Because this experimentation is more relevant to us than mindlessly repeating what doesn't work: breeding generations of artists, who religiously belief in self-expression and individualism but look the same, think the same, act the same. And whose work has no impact on their lives or the lives of the people around them.

We have used this manual in many different ways, from asking students to choose exercises to picking a random page number and challenging ourselves to respond.

We have used it in a rush, on the bus to the next teaching gig, desperate for inspiration. We have sent parts of this manual to our friends, when they asked: 'Got any quick advice on exercises or practices or games etc that are good for loosening tension in a group?'

We have used it as a prop to start discussions about why the institutions we teach in are so white, so exclusive, so untransparent.

We have used the manual

as a talisman, shielding behind it when we didn't feel confident enough to stand in front of a class, once again suffering from imposter syndrome.

We have flipped through this manual, when we were stuck, when we wanted to cancel, but couldn't afford to.

We have got out this manual when we wanted to use the potential of a group. We have used this manual to take collective shortcuts.

As we said in the beginning, this is an incomplete manual. We would like to hear about your own learning methods, ideas and experiences. This will certainly not be the last edition of his manual, and it would be good to know what we could add, leave out or change.

Just email us.

Editors:
mirjam.bayerdoerfer@gmail.com
rosalie.schweiker@gmail.com

Designer:
mdbhuntley@gmail.com

Rearrange the room you are in, examining the furniture and the logic of its placement

IKEBANA

Show each other your passports

CONTROL

Make a salad

THE ALISON EXERCISE

Walk to the next library
Choose a book each, referring to a given topic or personal interest
Choose a quote and read it to the group
Discuss the quotes or leave

THE NEXT LIBRARY

Invent a myth, e.g. how did the sun come into being?

Write it down

Illustrate it

BIG BIRD

Do something, go somewhere, eat something, look at something

Do the same activities on at least 3 consecutive days

Repeat with care

No deviations allowed

SPIRAL WORKSHOP

One person copies or makes up random captions
Another person takes photos
Match photos to captions

COPY & PASTE

Make a chore wheel

COLLECTIVE ACTIVISM

For a set amount of time take it in turns to come up with rules for moving as a group, inside or outside a building

V FORMATION

Split your teaching fee with the students

Each student gets a fraction of the full amount and can spend it on whatever they want

Talk about what you did with the money

ROBIN HOOD

Wash each other's feet

HABEMUS PAPAM

Bring an application
you wrote
Read it out aloud to
the group

OLD FLAMES (1)

Bring an unsuccessful application

Read it out aloud to the group and discuss why it was so good they didn't pick you

OLD FLAMES (2)

Truth or dare

PLAY

For each letter of the alphabet write down a term that comes to mind

Share your alphabet

Extra: Make a font with your own bodies

A TO Z

Think of somebody whose work you don't like

Write them an email to explain what you don't like about their work

Decide collectively if the email should be sent

ART CRITIC

Read a text together aloud

One person starts reading and stops when they don´t want to read anymore

Another person picks up where they stopped

Don't go around in a circle, be patient and accept the silence/ confusion

TRUST

Write down all your
phone numbers but don't assign
them names

Each of you takes one phone
number that isn't theirs

Go outside and do something

Call each other

TELEPHONE JOKER

Connect a phone to a speaker and call one phone number after the next, passing the telephone around, doing tutorials

TELEPHONE JOKER WITH TUTORIALS

Make a children's toy

NOT EASY

Compile a list of people you'd rather have as teachers than the ones you currently have

IF YOU'RE SO CLEVER, WHY DON'T YOU TEACH THE CLASS

One person in the group does everyday chores, e.g. going shopping, doing the washing up

The rest of the group observes

Take turns

EVERYDAY THEATRE

Write down 10 statements, e.g. I like my grandmother

In the classroom, mark one place as YES / I agree and another one as NO / I don't agree

Get everybody to stand in a line

Read out the statements and ask people to move depending on if they agree, disagree or aren't sure about the statements

LEFT / RIGHT

Pair up and give each other a simple task

You have 15 minutes to accomplish the tasks

Bring back the result or proof of having completed the task

TASKS

Invent and design a card game

ARTS & CRAFTS (1)

Invent and design a currency

ARTS & CRAFTS (2)

Make your own clothes

ARTS & CRAFTS (3)

Put on a puppet show
for children

ARTS & CRAFTS (4)

Put on a puppet show
for adults

ARTS & CRAFTS (5)

Move through a building from top to bottom or bottom to top

Look for places where you could set up your classroom and test them immediately

Take some chairs on your walk, if considered helpful

TOP DOWN
BOTTOM UP

Form a circle

Round 1: React to the first strong impulse for an action you can detect and do it, one after the other

Round 2: Repeat the action you did. Improvise, ping pong towards an instantly realisable action, responding to impulses from all members of the group, building up a group dynamic

Try to raise the level of complexity with every round you play

INSTANT GROUP DYNAMIC

Everybody brings 1kg of one type of material e.g. flour, oil, paper, concrete, ceramics, spaghetti, textile, peanut butter, confetti, duck tape, body lotion

Walk around a building or city

Try to lose your material along the way

Optional: trace your way back

WEIGHT LOSS

Jelly doesn't settle if there is
a kiwi in it
Draw a jelly bowl
Draw a kiwi in the jelly
Name the kiwi – what keeps
your jelly from settling?

THIS IS ALSO TRUE
FOR PINEAPPLES

Sing something together

Whoever does not know the words can hum

It also helps not to look at each other when you first start singing together

Close your eyes

C D E F G A H C

||: ToooMATensalat,
TomaTENsalat, TomatenSALat
TomatensaLAAAT,

ToMATensalat,
TomaTENsalat, TomatenSALat
TomatensaLAAAT :||

TRANSLATE THIS
SONG INTO YOUR
MOTHER TONGUES

Present someone's work without using a slide show or a projector

Instead work with the media the artist herself would use

PERFORMATIVE ARTISTS' TALKS

Everybody chooses an article, word or image that has something to do with them or their work

Introduce yourself/your work to the group with your chosen cutting

BUY LOTS OF NEWSPAPERS

Send every student a high res scan of your signature

NEW MEDIA

Open a restaurant
In a space that fits minimum
one person

OPEN A RESTAURANT

Be each other's interns

Assign internships by drawing names

Discuss and agree on working conditions for each internship

Formulate and sign contracts

INTERNSHIP LOTTERY

Choose a topic
Write down key elements relating to this topic
Use whatever you have at hand to represent these elements
Arrange a still life out of these objects
Interpret each other's compositions

STILL LIFE

Bring your computer

Allow each member of the group to open a fixed number of files of their choice

APPROPRIATION

Pair up

Write a text together, with one person using the keyboard and the other person using the mouse

Level 2: Move on to Photoshop

Swap roles from time to time

FANTASIA IN F MINOR FOR PIANO FOUR-HANDS

Take off a sock
Try to swap it with
someone else

TAKE OFF A SOCK

Walk as a group without speaking for at least 30 minutes

Decide who leads the walk nonverbally

Each of you should be the leader at some point

SILENT WALK

In a circle, hold hands

One person starts the ha: says ‘ha’ and passes it by squeezing their neighbours hand to the left

This is the prompt for the neighbour to say ‘ha’, then pass it on

‘Haha’ reverses the direction

Get a rhythm, see how fast you can go

PASS THE HA

Stand in a row
Clap as if you were
welcoming somebody on stage
One person walks in front
of the group
She says a sentence that
comes into her head
Everybody applauds
Clap somebody else on stage
Repeat until everybody has
had their applause

CLAP

Do something for a very long time without stopping, e.g. read a long book, watch all episodes of The Simpsons

Take turns, avoid pauses

Exceed the time limit

VERY LONG

Take off a sock and rub your foot with mustard
Pass the mustard around
Put the sock back on

MUSTARD

Swap clothes, if possible including make-up and shoes

Tell the person who is wearing your clothes what you have to do over the next days and what awaits you, but tell it as if she has to do it, e.g. "You will have to call your father. Get up at 7am. Buy spinach"

Everybody else listens

Repeat for everybody in the group

Keep on the clothes for as long as you can cope

THINK BEYOND
YOUR BODY

Imagine an utopian holiday destination

Interview each other in detail about this holiday (landscape, social life, accommodation, food, entertainment, sightseeing, cultural highlights)

Try not to describe Switzerland

ALL INCLUSIVE

Distribute the contents of your personal fruit bowl in a defined surrounding, e.g. your hotel room

Move on to the lobby once you get bored

THE TRAVELLING TEACHER

As a group stand closely together, facing one way

One splits off from the group, walks away, then runs back at them and crowd surfs

The others hold them up carefully

FLY

Re-invent yourself as a cartoon character

Make your costumes and at least one prop each

Stay in character for at least one day

COMIC

Invent a new sort of tea
Name it

JUST ADD HOT
WATER AND STIR

In a group, each of you picks two people

Move towards these two people to make the shape of an equilateral triangle

As each of you align with different people, keep trying

RELATIONAL AESTHETICS

Make a list of all the
buildings in your town where
bureaucratic power is located
Pay them a visit

LOCAL ADMIN POWER MAP

Each of you brings a recipe
for a meal that can feed the whole
group and is cheap

Every time you meet choose
a recipe and cook it

Publish your own cook book

FOOD

Don't start the class
Listen to the students chatting
See what happens

WHO BLINKS FIRST

Connect your phones to a projector
Show each other the images you store on your phones

CLOUD

Describe what each of you are wearing, your hairstyles and accessories

Write down and categorise

Next step: Go to an art event and do the same

Compare

ANALYSIS

Have someone give a presentation on a person and their work

Once the presentation is over the person enters the room

SURPRISE ENTRY

Go around the circle
Say who is better at doing x than you are, e.g. “Mirjam is better at cooking than I am”

COMPARISONS / COMPLIMENTS

Split into pairs
Draw each other's portraits
for 15 minutes each
Talking optional

DIALOGICAL PORTRAITS

Do a live drawing session
with the teacher as the nude model

TRADITIONAL ART
SCHOOL TECHNIQUES

As a group, go to
somebody's workspace
Arrange their workspace
according to your ideas

PUBLIC PLANNING

Everybody says their name
and what they had for breakfast

NOTHING

Cook a meal for everybody
Take out your credit or ID cards
Eat the meal using your cards as cutlery

MDMA

Decide on a leisure activity
to accomplish with the eagerness
and sincerity of your day job

Do your day job with an
expectation of fun and relaxation

SERIOUS FUN

Invite an expert to explain
how to do an effective tax return

USEFUL (1)

Ask an expert to visit you and explain your country's political system

USEFUL (2)

Learn how to code

USEFUL (3)

Design an invoice

USEFUL (4)

Go to the sauna together

USEFUL (5)

Bring your child(ren) to the lesson

USEFUL (6)

Collect invitation cards, flyers, brochures from your local art institutions and assess their gender balance

GUERRILLA GIRLS

Close your eyes
Imagine your life as a fairy tale
Write it down

ABSTRACTION EXERCISE

Swap social media profiles unannounced

AVATAR

Get together in pairs
Take 3 minutes each to make assumptions about the other person, saying them out aloud:

What hobbies do they have?
Where do they live?
Do they have children?
How do they vote?
What pets do they have?

Compare the assumptions with the facts afterwards, but not during

ASSUMPTIONS GAME

Research the history of art education in your region, country, continent

Give short presentations on your findings

WAYBACK MACHINE

Start a group discussion
After each contributor,
observe 10 seconds of silence

INTROVERT

Come up with different grading systems as a group

Write down criteria

Grade each other's work

Add written evaluations if it seems a fun thing to do

BACK TO NATURE

Bury some things that you think people in the future might find interesting

Bury them deep

FUTURE ARCHAEOLOGY

Make a list of buildings that are shut down or not used at a certain time or day of the week

Try to get into these buildings

VACANCY

Go around looking for wood, make a bonfire; if you have sausages grill them

GRILLAR KORV

Find local seasonal produce
Cook it

LOCAL (1)

Find local people that
interest you
Meet them

LOCAL (2)

Give a presentation about
your work in your local dialect

LOCAL (3)

Learn a local dialect

LOCAL (4)

Research interviews
with artists
Find the ones that interest
you and re-enact them

CANNIBALISM

Find things to do that you can do without spending money

CAREFREE

Everybody should pick at least one song

Make a playlist

Listen to this playlist whilst doing other things (e.g. working) and sing along

MAKE A PLAYLIST

Mimic a three legged race
but attach everyone's legs in a line
Try and work out how to
move together

WORK OUT

Go busking

FUNDRAISING

Make many different kinds of potato salad, embracing all the regional specialities

PROVINCIALISM

Make your own playdough
Sculpt your biggest fear

CONTEMPORARY CERAMICS (1)

Knead a lump of dough, covering your hands with a white cloth so you cannot see what you are doing

Decide whether peeking under other people's cloths is allowed

Bake and eat the sculpted shapes if you used edible dough

CONTEMPORARY CERAMICS (2)

Do something at night

NIGHT

Get a magazine
Choose a section, phrase or paragraph each
As a group, collage the parts together into one big read

READERS DIGEST

Get some paper and pens
Watch youtube videos of bands you like
Isolate a range of 'moves'
Name and illustrate them
Then perform them as a group

DO THE MOVES

Get everybody in the group crying

TOO SAD TO TELL YOU

Get a bunch of coconuts
Try to open them it with
whatever you can find

FORM AND CONTENT (1)

Get 4 tins of something
Split into 4 groups
Try to open the tins with anything but a tin opener
Once achieved, get together and compare methodologies

FORM AND CONTENT (2)

Talk about everything you've done for money in your life so far

BOOORING

Talk about the first thing you ever did for money

STARTER DRUG

Talk about your family and their relationship to money

Talk about the worst thing
you ever did for money

EAT SHIT

Talk about how much you pay for your studies
Talk about how much you get paid for teaching
Talk about the course budget

TRANSPARENCY

Each write down all the
words that have remained
unspoken
Mix them together in
someone's shoe
Reorder and talk about them
Add some words, take
some words
Sing the text together
Then shout the text together

MAKE A SONG

Go bra-less
Discuss what it means and
how it feels not to wear a bra

HANGING LOW

Pretend it's somebody's birthday

CELEBRATION

Make a list of all the languages spoken within your group

Translate parts of this manual into your mother tongues

AN ARTIST
WHO CANNOT
SPEAK ENGLISH
IS NO ARTIST

Scan this week's calendar
Project or print copies
Talk about the rhythm and diversity / monotony of your work schedule

LECTURE FOR THE SELF-EMPLOYED

Write down a list of of
actions and behaviours that would
terrify your mothers
Decide which of these
actions you should do now, as a
group

ALMA MATER

Every time somebody says
"art" take a sip of schnapps
Every time somebody says
"capitalism" take two

DRINKING GAME

Go swimming together

IMPROVISE

Think of somebody you truly admire

Discuss if it would be desirable to swap lives with this person

ENVY

Stand in a circle and take it in turns to make a sound that roughly expresses your mood at that moment

The whole group mimics it back

FEELING SOUNDS

Make an advert for something

ADVERTISING

Go on a boat trip together

PANTA RHEI (1)

Travel together to all four corners of the country

PANTA RHEI (2)

Cook a meal together
Then split the group in two
One group is the guests, one group is the waiters
Swap roles

DIVISION OF LABOUR

Turn your PhD into a zine

THE EDUCATIONAL TURN (1)

Turn your diploma into a paper aeroplane

THE EDUCATIONAL TURN (2)

Pick a subject

For 30 minutes each person writes down everything they know and feel about it

One thought per page

Share and discuss what you have written

Work together to map the writing on a wall

Observe the commonalities, differences and wider politics

SHARE THE FEELS

Choose an object

Tell everybody why you have chosen this object in 3 minutes

Tell everybody why you have chosen this object in 1 minute

Tell everybody why you have chosen this object in 1 word

EDITING

Read political party
programmes and policy papers

READING LIST

Cook spaghetti
While the spaghetti is boiling
use two pieces of dry spaghetti
as drumsticks and the rest of the
kitchen equipment as resonant
bodies

100 GREATEST
DRUMMERS
OF ALL TIME

Find a staircase

Everybody sits on a step

Move up slowly and silently, step by step

Don't talk

If anybody asks you what you are doing, the person sitting on the top step explains it

STEP BY STEP

Read a newspaper of your choice

Pick an article and write a letter to the editor

Post or email the letter

Repeat the exercise until your letter is published

SIR, ...

Wash each other's hair

WITH SHAMPOO

Write down your nickname on a name tag

Address each other by their nicknames for the rest of the seminar

KOSENAME

Exchange clothes with each other until everybody is wearing only one colour

Once sorted, the different colours then engage in a competition

UNIFORM

Write a new text for your national anthem and sing it at an official event

ENRICO PALAZZO

The class marches towards the sun in a row (one behind the other) until the sun has set

TOWARDS THE SUN

Before a session, each of you writes down one typical sentence often said in crits, e.g. "Have you thought about making it bigger?"

Everybody pulls one of these sentences out of a hat

Try to slip in your sentence during the crit without anybody noticing

At the end, show each other your sentences

GROUP CRIT

Prepare for this exercise by not sleeping the night before

Bring all the materials needed for a good and deep sleep to class

Sleep for the duration of the class

ZZZZZZZZZZZZZZ

Talk about what it was like to give birth

If nobody in your group has given birth, ask somebody who has given birth to come and talk to you about it

LIKE SHITTING A WATERMELON

Talk about what it was like to have an abortion

If nobody in your group has had an abortion, ask somebody who has had one to come and talk to you about it

30% HAPPY, 30% DEVASTATED AND 40% CONFUSED

The teacher hides in the school grounds

As soon as the teacher is found, the lesson starts

Repeat weekly

HIDE AND SEEK

On Mother's Day draw appropriate pictures on each others' bodies

MOTHER'S DAY

Write down sentences or phrases that you or your teacher use a lot (e.g. "Can somebody open the window please")

Replace each sentence with a number (e.g. "Can somebody open the window please" becomes "24")

Try to substitute more and more sentences with numbers

SHORTCUTS

Try to criticise each other's
work with a single noise

OH-OOOONNNNNAHH
ARRRRGGGGHHHHH
– KAPOWW

Walk to school slowly
enough to arrive just in time for
the last lesson of that day

AIR BREATHING
LAND SNAILS

Everybody in the group keeps an automatic diary for a week

At the end of the week everyone chooses their favourite slogan/phrase and writes it on a t-shirt

Put the t-shirts on a rail

Everyone takes one shirt

UNREASONABLE THOUGHTS

For the duration of the course, try not to read, quote or reference white European artists, academics, designers etc

DON'T USE
THIS MANUAL

Build a sparkling wine tower
Start with a solid table for
your tower's base. Place 10 glasses
in a square at the bottom
The next level is 9 glasses,
then 8, and so on
Make sure each glass
touches its neighbouring glasses
Once the tower is assembled,
slowly pour the sparkling wine

TRICKLE DOWN

Introduce yourself in relation to two points in time

One in the past and one in the future

Be specific about the time, e.g. I am 52 now – Twenty years ago, I got my first permanent contract as a lecturer – In five years time, I will retire

TIMELINE

Ask everybody to give a short presentation about what they would do, if they hadn't become an artist

If you already work in other professions than art, talk about those

ALTERNATIVES

Talk about emotional and domestic labour

Try to map who does what in your household

IT STARTS WHEN YOU SINK IN HIS ARMS, IT ENDS WITH YOUR ARMS IN HIS SINK

Stop using social media for
an hour, a day, a week or longer
Talk about your experiences

ADDICTION

In pairs, turn back to back
Bend your knees, find your
point of balance and rest on
each other
Lose control of your arms
Move your legs like you are
drunk and stay balanced back
to back

DRUNK

Go to the woods and find
a soily patch
Bring plaster and water
Find dips and marks, dig
holes and thrust in your fingers
Take casts of the marks
Wait for them to set
and remove
Arrange and leave as a
gift to the woods

DIRTY

Go to a shop that sells cosmetics and take some bits of paper with you

Test the shop's sample lipsticks and then make drawings of each other with the lipstick

SAMPLES

Go to the potato section of
your local supermarket
Find out where the potatoes
come from or who the farmer is
Go and meet them

PRODUCERS

Cut each others' hair

NON, JE NE
REGRETTE RIEN

Take a piece of paper
On one side write some words that describe the self you project externally
On the other side write some words that describe aspects of yourself you hide or don't show
Share your masks

MASKS

As a group come up with a set of 10 rules on how you want to spend your time together

1 – 10

Rearrange the seating order over and over, according to zodiac sign, age, colour of hair, number of siblings, etc.

PATTERNS (1)

Leave the building and collect whatever you can find: pebbles, leaves, trash

Return and put everything you brought on a table, one after the other

Study what you have collected, try to describe it

PATTERNS (2)

Walk around your area and photograph or draw different fonts you see

Try to come up with a new typeface based on what you have found

PATTERNS (3)

Everybody brings a piece of fruit to class

Describe yourself according to the fruit's attributes

Relate the pieces of fruit to each other, compare

Eventually, put them all in a blender

Share the smoothie

JUICY FRUIT

Produce one kilo of salt
dough per person
Work with this salt dough
over the course of one year
To keep it fresh, freeze it

SURROGATE

Attach an object to the ceiling using a bit of string

Sit down and form a circle around it

Give it a push and wait until it has finished dowsing

CENTRE OF ATTENTION

Choose one word, sentence
or motto that means something
to you
Embroider the chosen text

HOMEWORK

Invite people you don’t like to join you in producing a seasonal pesto made from local herbs

HEALING HERBS

Pair up

One person asks the other: What did you have for breakfast? What are your shoes made of? and similar questions

The interviewed person is only allowed to answer “wurst”

Swap roles when the interviewed person starts laughing

GERMAN HUMOUR

Go to a local archive

Silently split up and follow your noses

After 2 hours come together and report back on what each of you have found and what led you to it

RUMMAGING

Give passport photos
of yourself to cashiers at super-
markets as a gift

SPECIAL OFFER

Go to see your professor at her office and ask if you can tidy up her desk

THE ORDER OF THINGS

Each identify a skill that
you have
Teach them to each other

Buy a McDonalds meal
Work out the the ingredients
Try to cook it from scratch

FAST FOOD

Week 1: Watch and read nothing but news for the whole week

Week 2: Find the oldest possible documents on issues related to last week's news

Week 3: Go to a newspaper archive, choose a random week from the past and read as much as possible

Week 4: Read last week's news

Week 5: Follow your own news interests and find individuals or a group who share these interests

YESTERDAY'S NEWS

Use each other's apartments as work spaces

THE ARCHITECT AND THE HOUSEWIFE

Find something you'd like to know more about or a skill that you'd like to learn

Try to find other people who are interested in learning about the same things

Don't rush this

AGONISE AND ORGANISE

Wait for the bus or tram

As the public transportation vehicle approaches and opens its doors, stay where you are and don't get in

Repeat

DECISIONS

Craft animal head masks
Spend the day wearing and swapping masks

HORSING AROUND

In each region of Germany,
visit a hardware store
Test their restaurants

BAUMARKT

Compliment a stranger in public on an article of clothing they are wearing, their hair style, the book they are reading or what they are buying at the grocery store

CREEP

Find a comfortable place in public space

Dress appropriately for the weather

Write down everything you see, imagining you are watching a movie

1.000.000 MOVIES

Study the social security system of your country

Compare it to those of other countries

BENEFITS

Choose a meaningful object among your possessions

Write a story about the object based on your relationship to it

Ask a friend or relative to write a story about the same object

STUFF

Say Hi to everybody you
meet, even if you don’t know them
Don’t say Hi to anybody,
even if you know them

ALL DAY LONG

Spread the rumour that your performance class involves taking a shitload of drugs

EVERGREEN (1)

Read artists' obituaries
together
Vote on the most fun and
the most depressing one

EVERGREEN (2)

Try to do a serious crit on each others' Instagram feeds

LIKE

Spread the rumour that most "successful" artists you met are wildly unhappy

Skip class unannounced
For the next meeting, write
down what you did instead

COVER UP

Spend the whole weekend
together, including nights
If possible, go clubbing

AS A GROUP

Pull names from a hat
Write about each other's
work

MAGIC TRICK

Spread the rumor that you're willing to do 48 hour crits

IF YOU'RE UP FOR IT, DO IT!

Decide on a question you want to discuss or a subject about which to collect ideas

Take a few big pieces of paper

Some people start writing ideas and responses on the paper, then passes them onto the next person

They add their thoughts and pass it on until the paper is full.

Read the writing out loud

EXQUISITE CORPSE

In pairs, lie down while the other person sits nearby

Make gentle contact with each other (hold hands, touch shoulders)

Tell each other stories about the two of you in the future

THIS IS HOW WE WILL DIE

Talk about what you were like as teenagers

TIE-DYE

Mid-course, start pretending
to have an assistant who schedules
your meetings
See if the dynamic changes

MISS MONEYPENNY

Say “I don’t know” a lot

SMART ARSE

Split into small groups

Decide on a public place, e.g. shop, elevator, bus

Go to this place and do some research: What can this place teach us? What might be learnt here?

Meet again as the whole group and share your findings

MY VERY EXCELLENT MOTHER JUST SENT US NINE PIZZAS

Participate in a protest
you're not really interested in
Write slogans in a language
you don't understand

CUCKOO POLITICS

If there are one or more name-droppers in the class, pretend not to know who they're talking about

MARCEL DU-WHO?

Everybody brings an email that they consider the most important email they ever received

Stage a public reading of those emails

NEEDLE IN A HAYSTACK

Talk in a funny voice

EXPOSE

Pair up and take off
your shoes

One person stands still

The other person stands in
front of them and bends down to
put their hands on the tops of
their feet

Press the feet into the
ground. Swap after a while

MONUMENT

Do karaoke together

EXTROVERT

Take everybody on a trip to a shooting stand

If you can, bring self-made targets

SOCIAL DESIGN

If you aren't lazy: pretend to be lazy

If you are lazy: talk about being lazy

WORKAHOLIC

Work on a choir rendition of "Money Power Glory"

5:07

The teacher uses the furniture to block the entrance to the classroom

Once the students have managed to get in, start the lesson by rearranging the furniture

ENTRY POINT (1)

The students use the furniture to block the entrance to the classroom

Once the teacher has managed to get in, start the lesson by rearranging the furniture

ENTRY POINT (2)

In teams, walk across the field and back, erasing your traces on the way back

The winning team is the one which has left the least obvious traces, or the most creative ones

FIND A SMALL FIELD WITH UNTOUCHED SNOW

Arrange your chairs in two circles, one inner circle and one outer circle

The inner circle discusses an issue, the outer circle listens

After a set amount of time, swap circles and continue the discussion

At the end, come together in one circle and discuss the discussion

META

Incorporate an anecdote that happened to you on public transport into each teaching session

ANECDOTES

Each person finds a different solution for how you are arranged in the space when doing presentations, e.g. the presenter stands on the table and the audience sit under the tables

ON THE TABLE

Have conversations or tutorials while walking

BASIC

Take part in or organise
LARP

ROFL

Draw candle flames

HOWEVER MUCH YOU'LL TRY, IT'LL ALWAYS LOOK LIKE VAGINAS

Think of a body exercise that once helped you and share it with the rest of the group

HELP ME HELP YOU

Take a seat or chair into the public realm

Invite people to sit on it and share their wisdoms

Prepare questions in case prompts are necessary

CLICHÉS

Go out and get everything
you need for a coffee break
Have a coffee break

HERE AND NOW

Watch documentary films in somebody's living room

Move to another house for each documentary

DOLBY SURROUND

Make your own playdough
Sculpt yourself a souvenir to
remind you of the seminar / course

SOUVENIR

Bring the postal voting forms
for the next election and fill them
in together
Discuss your choices

BRIEFWAHL

Pair up

Start a fight

Stop when someone gets a black eye

Grade the quality of the colour gradient and the swelling

BACK TO NATURE II

Everybody puts their learning materials into a backpack

The person who walks for the longest time or distance wins the race

Whoever drops out starts reading aloud their learning materials, amplified by the speakers of the sports stadium

RACE

Bring unwanted clothes
or fabric
Spend the afternoon making
costumes
When you’re done,
go somewhere and perform
something

COSTUMES

In pairs discuss a range of big concepts housed in single words i.e. sex, charity, dissensus

Take notes and really listen

Feedback to the group but only share other peoples' ideas, not your own

AUTHORITY SHIFTS

Announce that the main goal of the class is to become friends

PRIORITIES

Go blackberry picking
Use the berries to mark your faces
Use your marked faces to make drawings

WITH PAPER

Go for a silent walk
As a group collect 10 objects
Bring them back and silently
create a display of your findings
Write stories about how each
thing got to where you found it

TAXONOMY

Spend your entire course budget on blank photocopies

Put the pile in the classroom and work with its potential

Use handwriting as much as possible

GOING BLANK

Flip through this book and vote on which ideas you'd like to take forward

SUPERPEDA-
GOGICALIEXPI-
ALIDOCIOUS

Everybody brings their toothbrushes

The teacher squeezes a small amount of toothpaste on each toothbrush

Brush your teeth together

FAREWELL

Teaching for people
who prefer not to teach
Fourth edition (2023)

Edited by
Mirjam Bayerdörfer
and Rosalie Schweiker
Designed by
Margherita Huntley
Printed by
Tallinn Book Printers

People who more or
less consciously contributed
to this manual
Mariann Oppliger
Eva Weinmayr
San Keller

Stefan Burger
Alison Knowles
Kerri Jefferis
Emmet Williams
Chantal Küng
John Baldessari
Fischli & Weiss
Rosalie Schweiker
Pablo Helguera
Doris Stauffer
Sonia Boyce
Flick Allen
Micha Bonk
Katharina Ritter
Max Grau
Athena Vida
Nina Power
Frédéric Ehlers

Daniel Marti
Lily Wittenburg
Rebecca Fortnum
Josie Sutcliffe
Philip Matesic
Thomas Pausz
Mirjam Bayerdörfer
Andrea Francke
Clemens Krümmel
Robert Esterman
Roland Roos
Jacob Wren
Romy Rüegger
RELAX
(chiarenza & hauser & co)
Sophie Chapman
Giles Bunch
Katherine Fishman

Alexis Martinis Roe
Valeria Graziano
Shiri Shalmy
Nina Gasteva
Chto Delat
Ellie Wyatt
Amy Franceschini
Peter Strickmann
Naomi Liesenfeld
Sophie Hofer
Martina Wegener
Res Thierstein
Karin Sander
The students at the School of Barbiana
Alexandrina Hemsley

Thank you

The editors would especially like to thank

Berggasthaus Aescher, Appenzell

David Morris

Romy Rüegger

RELAX (chiarenza & hauser & co)

Ulf Aminde

Stuart Whipps

AltMFA

Eva Weinmayr

Søren Hansen and Jesper Jensen and everybody else who made the Little Red Schoolbook happen

Published by AND

ISBN 978-1-907840-12-8